Wash your hands!
Scrub them clean!

Tiny germs cannot be seen.

They hide.
They creep
beneath the nails.

They have eyes,
feet, and tails.

A Rookie reader®

Germs

Written by Judy Oetting
Illustrated by Tad Herr

Children's Press®
A Division of Scholastic Inc.
New York • Toronto • London • Auckland • Sydney
Mexico City • New Delhi • Hong Kong
Danbury, Connecticut

I dedicate this book to all children.
Please remember: A healthy lifestyle leads
to a happy, productive life.
—J.O.

For my mother, who always considered my
cluttered room a potential breeding ground
for all the little critters in this book.
—T.H.

Reading Consultant

Eileen Robinson
Reading Specialist

Library of Congress Cataloging-in-Publication Data
Oetting, Judy.
  Germs / written by Judy Oetting; illustrated by Tad Herr.
     p. cm. — (A Rookie reader)
  ISBN 0-516-24980-0 (lib. bdg.)   0-516-24995-9 (pbk.)
  1. Hygiene—Juvenile literature. 2. Microorganisms—Juvenile literature. I. Herr,
Tad, 1952- II. Title. III. Series.
  RA780.O38 2006
  613'.0432—dc22

                              2005016146

CHILDREN'S PRESS, and A ROOKIE READER®, and associated logos are trademarks and/or
registered trademarks of Scholastic Library Publishing. SCHOLASTIC and associated logos
are trademarks and/or registered trademarks of Scholastic Inc.
1 2 3 4 5 6 7 8 9 10 R 15 14 13 12 11 10 09 08 07 06

Beware! They're there!

Lick your fingers.
Chew your nails.

Germs in your mouth
will never fail.

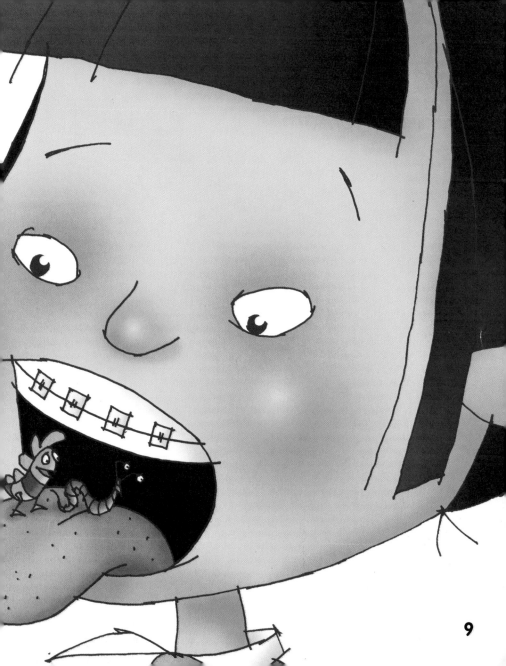

Down the tummy they will go.

They'll have lots of fun below.

Beware! They're there!

Cover your mouth
before you sneeze.

Germs travel fast
to spread disease.

Faster than
cheetahs or
speeding cars!

Run away!
Go very far!

Beware! They're there!

19

Wash hands!
Scrub them!
Keep them clean.

Germs are bad.
Germs are mean.

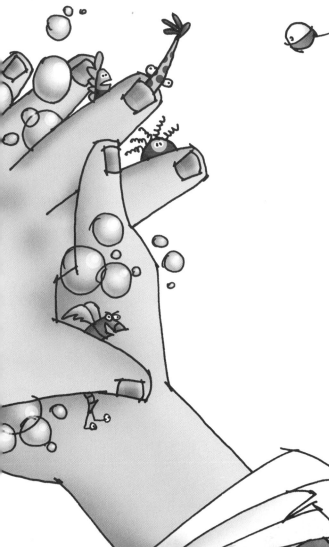

Yucky germs
cannot be seen.

Wash fingers
in between.

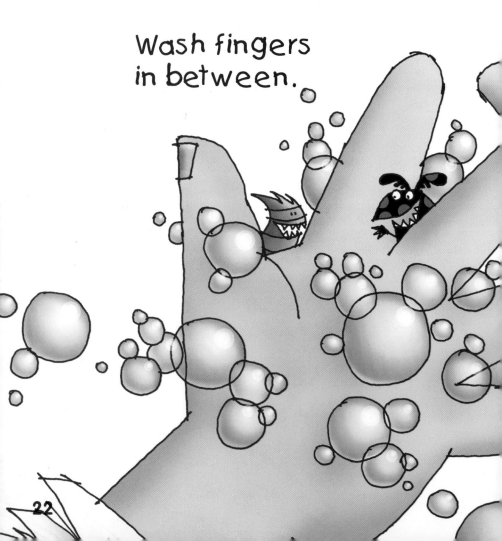

Beware! They're there!

Wash your hands.
Don't spread disease.

Wash them often.
Use soap, please!

It's important that you do.

Don't forget! Dry them, too!

Germs are everywhere!

Word List (79 Words)
(Words in **bold** are story words that rhyme.)

and	creep	germs	often	they
are	**disease**	**go**	or	they'll
away	**do**	hands	**please**	they're
bad	don't	have	run	tiny
be	down	hide	scrub	to
before	dry	important	**seen**	**too**
below	everywhere	in	**sneeze**	travel
beneath	eyes	it's	soap	tummy
between	**fail**	keep	speeding	use
beware	**far**	lick	spread	very
cannot	fast	lots	**tails**	wash
cars	faster	**mean**	than	will
cheetahs	feet	mouth	that	you
chew	fingers	**nails**	the	your
clean	forget	never	them	yucky
cover	fun	of	**there**	

About the Author

Judy Oetting taught school for 33 years. She loves writing children's books, and presents programs in science and nature for schools, libraries, and the Burr Oak Woods Conservation Department. Judy was born on September 24th, 1936, and lives in Levasy, Missouri. She's healthy and wants you to be healthy, too.

About the Illustrator

Tad Herr has been an illustrator and graphic designer for more than 30 years. He lives in an old log house in Lancaster County, Pennsylvania. He spends much of his time in the studio buried under piles of sketches until his wife lures him away with promises of cookies and strawberry popsicles.

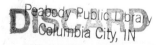